BE STILL

A TREATMENT AGAINST FEAR

Emmet Fox

This book is protected by copyright, and you can't copy any part of it without getting permission first. The author's opinions in the book are their own, and they might not be the same as the Publisher's opinions.

© Copyright 1994 by Snowball Publishing

www.snowballpublishing.com

info@snowballpublishing.com

THE Bible teaches spiritual Truth in many different ways. It gives direct teaching about God, as clear and precise as any book on philosophy that ever was written. It expounds the Great Message indirectly through historical narrative and by means of biographical studies, for the Bible includes the most wonderful and interesting set of human biographies that ever was written. It contains an unmatched collection of essays and treatises on the nature of God, and the nature of man, the powers of the soul, and the meaning of life.

But it is in its prayers and treatments that the Bible is transcendent. It contains a large number of the greatest prayers ever written—beginning, of course, with what we call the "Lord's Prayer"—prayers the like of which have never been found elsewhere, for they go right down to the depths of the human soul, meeting every need that can arise, and providing for every possible temperament and any conceivable contingency —in fact they cater to "all sorts and conditions of men." Among all the beautiful and heart-searching prayers of the Bible there is none that surpasses the wonderful poem that we call the Forty-Sixth Psalm.

This is an inspired treatment that will enable you to overcome any kind of difficulty; if you can tune yourself in to the level of consciousness to which it attains. It is the supreme Bible treatment, against fear.

Now the object of prayer or treatment is just this very raising of the consciousness, and a good prayer is the instrument that enables us to do it. We need not expect to begin our prayer with a realization. If we already had a realization we should not be needing the help of the prayer; we do not need a step-ladder to reach a height on which we are already placed. The ladder is employed in order to enable us to raise ourselves, step by step, to a height above the ground to which our muscles alone would never carry us ; and so a good prayer is a step-ladder upon which we may gradually climb from the low level of fear, doubt, and difficulty, to the spiritual height where these things melt away in the Light of Truth. Our psalm begins, as do nearly all the Bible prayers, with an expression of faith in God. This is extremely important in practice. You need to affirm constantly that you do believe in God, not merely as a vague abstract concept, but as a real, vivid, actual power in life, always available to be, contacted in thought; never changing and never failing.

It cannot be too strongly emphasized that it is not sufficient to take this for granted. It is not sufficient to accept the Truth once and for all, or once a week; you must continually reaffirm it in thought, and words if necessary. You must constantly remind yourself that you do accept this position, that you believe in it, and that your conviction is good enough to build your life and your hopes upon.

All this is treatment, and very powerful treatment too. It is treatment that really changes the soul by clearing out those subconscious fears that are the cause of all your difficulties.

And so, the inspired writer starts his prayer by saying, bluntly, God is our refuge and strength, a very present help in trouble. You will see that he allows himself no doubts at all about this. He does not dream of taking up the timid, almost apologetic, attitude that some modern divines seem to think appropriate in dealing with God.

He says firmly that God IS, that He exists indeed; and then he enumerates three facts concerning God. He says that He is our refuge; he says that He is our strength; and he says that He is "a very present help in trouble." This verse is really tremendous, is it not ? If we get through the crust of familiarity that tends to hide the real meaning from us, and study these words with a fresh mind, we shall be amazed, I think, at all that they imply. Note that he says that God is our refuge. He does not say that such may very well be the case, or that it is a pious hope upon which we are justified in leaning; but that, plain and plump, God is our refuge.

Now pause a moment to consider all that God is. Review briefly, at this point, the principal aspects and attributes of God as you know them, and then consider that this Infinite Being is our refuge. That is to say, this Unlimited Power of Wisdom and Love is a refuge to which we can go in any kind of difficulty. Many devout souls have thought of God as a distant potentate

dwelling in the skies, to the dreaded and feared; but the Bible says on the contrary that God is a refuge for those in difficulty. It then says that this Omnipotent Power is nothing less than our strength. This brings the idea home still more vividly. God is not merely a matchless power that will come to our rescue, but He will actually be our own strength, operating through us to the overcoming of difficulty when we call upon Him in the right way.

Every student of Truth must understand that God always acts through us by changing our consciousness.

We learn in divine metaphysics that God never does anything to us, or for us, but always through us. The writer drives these points home in the familiar Bible manner by adding, "a very present help in trouble." The opening affirmation is followed, in the most scientific way, by an excellent example of the use of what is called in metaphysics the "denial."

The next two verses are a denial that there is any power in conditions to make us be, or do, or submit to, anything short of the complete all-round harmony that is the Divine Will for us all. It says therefore will not we fear—as following logically upon our opening affirmation— though the earth be removed, and though the mountains be carried into the midst of the sea; Though the waters thereof roar and be troubled, though the mountains shake with the swelling thereof.

The "earth," of course, means manifestation. It is the Bible's term for all one's manifestation, or expression— the body, the home, the business life, relatives and associates, all come under the heading of the earth or the land. We know that all these outer things are but the expression of inner states of consciousness, and here the Psalmist makes us say that though the earth be removed, though all these outer things seem to go to pieces, our health break down, our money disappear, our friends desert us, yet we are not going to be afraid. This attitude is extraordinarily valuable.

When things are going wrong declare constantly that you are not going to be afraid or intimidated by any outer condition. The more afraid you find yourself; the more need is there for doing this. The most important time to say, "God is my refuge, I am not going to be afraid," is when your knees are knocking together.

The Psalmist says that though the mountains be carried into the midst of the sea, and the waters roll and tremble until the very mountains themselves seem to shake, he is not going to be afraid. The mountain, in the Bible, always means prayer, the uplifted consciousness, and this clause makes us declare that even when in the midst of our prayers things seem to get worse, so that the very prayers themselves are all but swamped by our terror, or doubt, or, despair; yet we are going to hold on to the truth about God, knowing that even though it be after forty days, the waters will subside—if only we hold on to the thought of God. The waters, of course, are always the human personality, and more especially the emotions.

The man who wrote this, we will agree, had no small knowledge of the human heart, its difficulties, and its needs.
There is a river, the streams whereof shall make glad the city of God, the holy place of the tabernacle of the Most High. This is the capital river mentioned several times in scripture; the river of life that flows from the throne of God. It means the understanding of Truth that is verily the "Waters of Life" to those who to those who attain it. The river as a symbol is rather interesting. Primarily

it stands for purpose. A river means purpose because it is always going somewhere.

A river does not stay in one place, like a lake, or even an ocean, but is always on the way to a destination. In this respect it is a true type of the dedicated life which every student of Divine Truth is supposed to be living. In this teaching, if it really means anything to us, we are no longer drifting about like a log at the mercy of the tide, but are definitely headed along the pathway of understanding and freedom.

"The City of God" is man's consciousness. Your consciousness, which is your identity in life, is called a "city" in the Bible. "Except the Lord keep the city, the watchman wakes but in vain." Now the consciousness in which the Light of Truth begins to shine again after an attack of fear or unhappiness, is a city purified by that holy river, and it becomes a glad city, a city of God or good, a holy place for the tabernacles of the Most High. God is indeed in the midst of such a city, and when God, which is to say, our realization of God, is in the midst of our consciousness, then truly we shall not be moved.

God is in the midst of her; she shall not be moved: God shall help her, and that right early. Here the Psalmist adds one of those simple touches, expressed in the most direct and childlike language, that go straight to the heart. He says "God shall help her—and that right early." This beautiful promise should remove the last traces of fear and doubt that may linger in the dark corners of the soul.

The metrical rhythm of the poem is preserved by a reiteration of the general theme in the next verse. The heathen raged, the kingdoms were moved: he uttered his voice, the earth melted. The heathen, needless to say, means your own wrong thoughts, those fears, doubts, self-reproaches, and shortcomings of every kind that come between you and your realization of God—the heathen forces that attack the holy city of your soul, sometimes lay siege to it for days and weeks, and sometimes even capture and occupy it for a time. Only for a time, however, if you hold steadfastly to God by constant prayer, for sooner or later, as surely as God lives, the kingdom of error shall be moved. He will "utter his voice" through your prayers and affirmations, and your salvation will come.

The third and last stanza of our treatment is an exercise of thanksgiving and praise. These Bible treatments are constructed with the utmost care and in the most scientific way. Usually, though not always, for there must be no hard and fast rules in prayer, they begin with an affirmation of faith in God. Then they analyze fear and worry, showing that God has no part in such things, and that we, therefore, need not fear them. They go on to remind us of the love and power and wisdom of God, and of our ability, as the children of God, to call upon His power in any kind of danger or trouble. They make these truths vivid to us with unexcelled literary skill, using the most diverse images and examples to that end; arid then they commonly finish, as prayers nearly always should, with a song of praise and thanksgiving.

Now the Psalmist makes us say The Lord of hosts is with us: the God of Jacob is our refuge. This destroys the feeling of God being afar off. The "Lord of Hosts" is the title for God that stresses His great power and might. It is the omnipotence aspect of God, we should say technically. So here we declare that Omnipotence is with us, and working through us; and he carefully adds that it is also God of Jacob. Now Jacob stands for the soul that is not yet redeemed, the soul still struggling in difficulty and conscious imperfection. Israel, "the Prince of God," is the soul that has realized its divine nature; but Jacob is still in the midst of his troubles. So, the Psalmist here reminds us that God is the Great Power, the Lord of Hosts, for Jacob just as well as for Israel.

Come, behold the works of the Lord, what desolations he hath made in the earth. He maketh wars to cease unto the end of the earth; he breaketh the bow, and cutteth the spear in sunder; he burneth the chariot in the fire. Here he continues with thanksgiving, saying, in effect:

Let us consider the power and the glory of this God who is always with us; how his action in prayer transforms our conditions, and makes desolate, or destroys, our troubles and worries; how He makes the wars—a splendid name for that worrying and stewing in misery that blights the lives of so many people—to cease in every part of our consciousness; how he disarms all the things of which we are afraid, not just putting them out of the way for the time being, but absolutely destroying any power they ever had. When you captured an enemy regiment in those days, smashed their bows and their spears, and burned their chariots, you had put them out of action pretty completely. That regiment could never trouble you again.

Be still, and know that I am God: I will be exalted among the heathen, I will be exalted in the earth. This really is probably the most wonderful phrase in the whole Bible. It really is the whole Bible in a nutshell. "Be still, and know that I am God." This is just the very last thing that we want to do when we are worried or anxious. The current of human thought that Paul calls the carnal mind is hurrying us along to its own ends, and it seems much easier to swim with it by accepting difficulties, by rehearsing grievances, by dwelling upon symptoms, than to draw resolutely away in thought from these things, and contemplate God, which is the one way out of trouble.

Train yourself to rise above this hurrying tide of error—error is always hurried; to sweep you off your feet is its master strategy—and, turning your back upon conditions, however bad they may seem, be still and know that I am God.

Even in your prayers there is a time for vigorous treatment, and there is also a time to cease active work and, "having done all, to stand"—to be still and know that I am God.

This of course does not mean merely doing nothing, or going away to concern one's self with some secular thing such as reading a novel or a newspaper. It is being still to know that God is God. Such "stillness" is the reverse of laziness or inaction. The still dwelling upon God is the quietest but the most potent action of all.

The Lord of hosts is with us; the God of Jacob is our refuge. Here again metrical symmetry obliges the poet to close his wonderful poem with a repetition of the general theme. Spiritually, too, it is a most powerful and effective ending to our prayer. The God of power who helps weak and frail mortals in the day of trouble is working through us, and so all will be well.

Note: The word Selah is no part of the poem itself but a stage direction to the temple musicians who chanted the psalms as part of a liturgy.

Recommended Readings

Riches Are Your Right by Joseph Murphy

The Money Illusion by Irving Fisher

How To Win Friends And Influence People: A Condensation From The Book by Dale Carnegie

Praying the Psalms by Thomas Merton

The Magic of Believing by Claude M. Bristol

Scientific Advertising by Claude C. Hopkins

The Law of Success: Using the Power of Spirit to Create Health, Prosperity, and Happiness by Paramahansa Yogananda

Available at

www.snowballpublishing.com

www.ingramcontent.com/pod-product-compliance
Lightning Source LLC
LaVergne TN
LVHW042045070526
838201LV00077B/806